The FACT ATTACK series

Awesome Aliens
Beastly Bodies
Cool Cars
Crazy Creatures
Crucial Cricket
Dastardly Deeds
Deadly Deep
Devastating Dinosaurs
Dreadful Disasters
Fantastic Football
Gruesome Ghosts
Incredible Inventions
Mad Medicine
Magnificent Monarchs
Nutty Numbers
Remarkable Rescues
Rowdy Rugby
Spectacular Space
Super Spies
Vile Vampires

FACT ATTACK

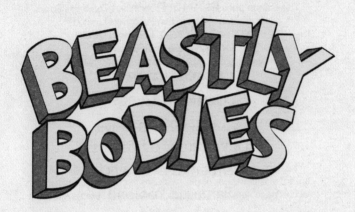

BEASTLY BODIES

IAN LOCKE

MACMILLAN CHILDREN'S BOOKS

First published 1998 by Macmillan Children's Books

This edition published 2012 by Macmillan Children's Books
a division of Macmillan Publishers Limited
20 New Wharf Road, London N1 9RR
Basingstoke and Oxford
Associated companies throughout the world
www.panmacmillan.com

ISBN 978-1-4472-2416-7

A CIP catalogue record for this book is available from
the British Library.

Printed and bound by CPI Group (UK) Ltd, Croydon CR0 4YY

DID YOU KNOW THAT . . .

 Captain Cook and his crew were the first British explorers to see tattoos. They saw them on the natives of the Pacific island of Tahiti, when they landed there in 1769.

 Victims of disasters can become diabetic for a short time – about ten days – as a result of shock.

 A woman celebrating her 100th birthday in Derbyshire in November 1996 overdid it – as a result she was taken to hospital for the first time in her life!

In a survey in January 1997, three per cent of those questioned in Britain said they had baths with their pets, and ten per cent ate snacks in the bath!

 In the twelfth century Henry 1 of England decreed that a yard was equal to the distance from the end of his nose to the end of his thumb when his arm was stretched out.

 While salt is important for people's health, too much salt can be dangerous. However, Chinese sports teacher Zhao-Cheng seems to stay healthy even though he eats a pound of salt a day.

 There is enough of the chemical phosphorus in a normal human body to make 2,200 matches!

A baby can get hiccups before it is born.

 From 13 June 1948 until 1 June 1949 a person in Los Angeles hiccuped 160 million times. People sent in 60,000 suggestions for cures. Vera Stone, aged 18, hiccuped for 59 days in 1929. Nothing she tried seemed to stop the attack. Her doctor thought she might have forgotten how to stop and decided to make her think of something else. He gave her a drug which made her feel ill but also put her to sleep. When Vera woke up she forgot to hiccup because she was paying attention to her other sickness. It did not take long for her to get better.

 Studies show that young women are more frightened of the dentist than men are.

Edwin Robinson was in a road crash which left him blind and almost unable to hear. His doctors said he would not get better. In June 1980, going out to check on his pet chicken at his home in America, he was struck by lightning and knocked out. He came to twenty minutes later and found he could see and hear. A month later he also found hair beginning to grow again on his bald head!

 You can catch the same cold several times over. A cold can be helped by eating curry.

 There are 2 square metres of skin on each fully grown body.

The bodies of Australian aborigines cannot deal with air conditioning. If they stay in a place with air conditioning they lose body heat and can die of cold.

Sometimes people appear to be dead but are not. One of the strangest cases was that of a 12-year-old girl in Wales. She was said to have "died" of pneumonia. She was laid out and put on a stretcher. As the bearers lifted the stretcher, she sat up and said, "Shut the door, it's cold." She went on to marry and have seven children.

 In north-west China in 1995, a dentist completed a three-metre tower from teeth he had taken out. He built it to frighten villagers into looking after their teeth.

In 1925 a young British girl was offered a country medicine for help with her whooping cough. It was a mouse boiled in milk!

 Babies can be born naturally or can be born by Caesarean section, when a cut is made in the mother to let the baby out. The name came from the son of the ancient Roman Emperor Julius Caesar, who is said to have been born in this way. This method of being born was not used in Europe again for hundreds of years. The first time it was re-used was in 1500 in Switzerland – the operation was carried out by a butcher! The first Caesarean operation in Britain took place in a hospital in Blackburn, Lancashire, in 1793.

 Caroline Clare of Canada is reported to have been magnetic. Knives and forks could be attached to her skin and stay there without any obvious help.

The first great outbreak of the bubonic plague, known as the Black Death, happened in Britain in June 1348, at Melcombe, Weymouth, in Dorset. By the time the plague was over, up to a quarter of the people in Europe had died.

 A British woman, Gillian McCarthy, is allergic to everyday chemicals. She gets ill if she smells petrol, cleaners, paint, perfume, newspapers, rubber and even tap water. If she smells these things she has headaches, becomes worn out and can faint.

 After his death in 1928, the heart of the British writer Thomas Hardy was stolen by a cat and never found.

The Pedaung women of Burma stretch their necks with large numbers of brass rings.

 During a terrific thunder and lightning storm in Arizona, USA, in 1929, the lightning lit up the eerie outline of a dark horseman, sitting absolutely still in his saddle out on the open plain. Once the storm had passed, a search party was sent out to find rancher Roy Sorrell. They found him – the man and his horse were standing stock-still on the plain. Both man and horse had been struck by a lightning bolt and killed; they remained "frozen" just as they had been when the lightning struck.

 Many people who are left-handed play golf, cricket and other games right-handed.

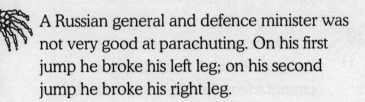

The tongue is the strongest muscle in the body. It is the only muscle which is attached at only one end.

A Russian general and defence minister was not very good at parachuting. On his first jump he broke his left leg; on his second jump he broke his right leg.

John Evans, a British builder, has a 23-inch neck. On 5 July 2008 he set a world record by balancing 98 milk crates on his head for 10 seconds.

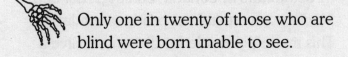

Only one in twenty of those who are blind were born unable to see.

9

A human can walk on water, with some help. Rémy Bricka of Paris walked across the Atlantic ocean wearing special skis, from April to May 1988. The distance he walked was 3,502 miles.

 A person's temperature can be lowered from 37 to 25 degrees centigrade without harmful effects.

 Diabetes is a disease in which people are unable to make insulin. It was first identified in Germany in 1889. It was found that the body makes insulin to control the amount of sugar in the body. Up to 1923 most of those who had diabetes died early. That year three doctors in Canada, Banting, Best and MacLeod, were able to produce insulin. This made it possible for diabetics to live a near-normal life with injections.

About 1771, Edward Jenner, an English student doctor, met a milkmaid in the country. She told him that she could not catch the disease smallpox because she had already had a mild form of the disease, cowpox, which she had caught from the cows she milked. Jenner decided this example might be repeated. He started to deliberately infect people with a mild form of a disease to prevent them catching a more serious infection. After experiments he found this idea of "vaccination" worked. By 1801 over 100,000 people had been vaccinated against smallpox in Britain. This success led to the use of vaccination across the world.

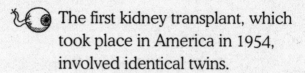 The first kidney transplant, which took place in America in 1954, involved identical twins.

 Elizabeth Blackwell, the first woman doctor of modern times (she died in 1910), was opposed to vaccination.

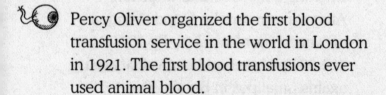 Percy Oliver organized the first blood transfusion service in the world in London in 1921. The first blood transfusions ever used animal blood.

Professor Christiaan Barnard of South Africa decided to try a heart transplant on a person in late 1967. In December he transplanted a girl's heart into the body of Louis Washkansky. Though his patient lived only eighteen days after the operation, Professor Barnard had proved a human heart transplant was possible.

A man in Wisconsin, USA, hibernated each winter for twenty-three years from November to Easter.

13

Ray Palmer is one of the leading photographers of rock stars in the world. Unusually he has only one good eye. Though his eyes look normal he was blind in one eye from the time he was born – it is likely he poked the eye by accident before he was born. Only when he was thirteen did he tell anyone else he could not see out of one eye.

 The strength of some people is extraordinary. An 18th-century strongman, Thomas Topham, could click his fingers while a man danced on each of his outstretched arms!

 Blood takes one minute to be pumped round the body and return to the heart.

A French monk who died in 1609 aged 70 only ate one meal a day for 48 years. It consisted of bread, water and a few raw roots.

By the time a person is 50, their nails will have grown a total of 2 metres.

 The big toe has only two bones, the other toes three. Webbed toes and fingers are quite common. The second and third toes often have extra skin which makes them webbed, usually on both feet.

 The nail on the middle finger grows fastest. The nail on the thumb grows slowest.

An adult human heart beats 60 to 70 times a minute. The heart of a baby beats about 130 times a minute. By the age of three the heart has slowed to 100 beats a minute, then down to about 90 a minute by the age of 12.

The actor Gary Cooper had big feet: he wore size 14 shoes. The imprints of his shoes and hands were made in the concrete outside Grauman's Chinese theatre in Hollywood. The world's most famous footprints – of Neil Armstrong, the American astronaut, on the Moon – are quite small: his boots were size 9 and a half.

Some people have a disease which means they cannot cry. The South African leader Nelson Mandela is one person who cannot cry. His many years in prison, where he broke rocks, stopped his eyes from making tears.

A hypochondriac is a person who believes they have something wrong with them all the time. British rock star and multimillionaire Dave Stewart has this. After he went to doctors he found there was never anything wrong with him. In the end he decided he was "ill" because he was very happy! He was said to have Paradise Syndrome. Once, when in Bangkok, Thailand, he had a healthy appendix removed because he thought it was diseased – he only had wind! He bought his own hospital in 1997 – the St Paul's Hospital in Covent Garden, London – and made it into an arts centre.

 Teeth do not stay still. They move in the mouth for most of a person's life. Tooth decay is the world's most common disease.

Children were not supposed to go near the corpses of plague victims in England in the sixteenth and seventeenth centuries. Some did not care. In London crowds of people, including children, stood at the open plague pits filled with dead bodies to show they were not frightened by the plague.

 Some well-known people ended up being buried in strange places. Both Emperor Selassie of Ethiopia, a hero to Rastafarians, and the great Indian poet Sheik Zauq, were buried under lavatories.

 You cannot tell the size of a woman's shoes by looking at the footprints they make. You have to look at her real foot or know how high her heels are.

Dutch giant Jan Van Albert was 2.87 metres tall in 1920.

 Siamese twins are called after Chang and Eng Bunker, who were born joined together in Siam (Thailand) in 1811. They were put on show in Europe and America. They lived to the age of 62. They married two sisters and had 22 children. They died within an hour of each other.

Many people have been said to live a long time. A Mr Agha of Kurdistan said he was 156 years old; he was probably about 75.

 Teeth are the only bits of a person which do not grow back. Charles Land of Detroit, USA, was the man who invented porcelain caps for broken teeth.

It is said that hair and nails continue to grow after death, but this is not true. When Admiral Lord Nelson was killed at the Battle of Trafalgar, near Spain in 1805, the British sailors on board his ship, the *Victory*, put his body in a coffin to take it home. (A dead sailor was usually thrown over the side into the sea, wrapped in a hammock or sack.) So that Nelson's body would not decay and smell horrible, it was put in alcohol. When his body was taken out back in England, it was said that his hair and nails had grown!

 The average person swallows 295 times while eating a meal. Until they are seven months old, babies can swallow and breathe at the same time.

Getting hot then cold can cause people to die. When there are hot summer days in Britain people can die because they have too big a shock from a change in temperature. Often the death is caused by jumping into icy cold water on very hot days to cool down. The most famous person to die in this way was Paul Morphy. He was a brilliant American chess player. One day, after walking in very hot weather, he decided to have a very cold bath. Soon after he got into his bath he died.

 A human can survive for about five weeks without food, about five days without water, but only for about five minutes without air. There are some extraordinary exceptions – Brian Cunningham of Jackson, Michigan in the USA, was revived after he had spent 38 minutes trapped underwater!

The heart in almost all humans is on the left side. When it turns up on the right, all the other internal bits are also moved from left to right. Some people can be very different. During World War One, an Australian soldier went to hospital for some trouble with a leg. He was found to have two hearts! They beat one after the other.

 On average the people of Liechtenstein live the longest in the world – a woman to over 82 and a man to over 77. On average a man in Britain will live to 71 and a woman to 77.

 Forty per cent of people in space suffer from space sickness.

 A sneeze can travel over 3.5 metres! The world speed record for a sneeze is 103 miles an hour.

The skin on the bottom of your feet is thicker than at any other place on your body. The average pair of feet will sweat about half a pint of perspiration a day. During a normal day a person will take about 18,000 steps. In an average lifetime, a person will walk the equivalent of almost three times round the world.

 The brain uses one fifth of all the oxygen we breathe.

 If calcium is taken out of human bones, they become so rubbery that they can be tied in a knot like rope or string.

 The fastest human has a speed of about 27 miles per hour, a racehorse about 60 miles per hour and a racing pigeon about 90 miles per hour.

The Russian Siamese twins Irina and Galiana had one torso, two arms, four legs and two heads. They were very different. One was calm, the other excitable. They had one nervous system and slept at different times. They were proof that sleep is controlled by the brain.

 The American cyclist Greg Lemond, winner of the world's toughest cycling race, the Tour de France, rode with 35 lead pellets in his body. He had been accidentally shot while hunting in 1987.

 One person in twenty has an extra rib.

A man's or boy's eyes are bigger than those of a woman or a girl, even if they are the same size.

In the 1890s it was the fashion for women to have very small waists. Some women had operations to take out their lowest ribs so they looked fashionable.

 Eskimos have extra flaps on their noses so they are not frozen when it is very cold.

 Lord Tennyson, the famous Victorian poet, did not kiss a girl until he was 41 years old. That was when he got married.

 In the 1970s it was found that some hard corals could be used to replace broken or chipped bones in people. The corals are so hard they last for many years and can be shaped to suit almost any type of bone.

A small injury can sometimes kill. William III (William of Orange) was out riding at Hampton Court when his horse Sorrel put his foot in a molehill and slipped. The king was thrown off the horse and broke his collarbone. The broken bone led to other illnesses and he died.

 Most babies who are born premature are left-handed.

 Jack Le Laune was known as Mr Keep Fit in the USA. In 1974, when he was 60, he swam from Alcatraz, which used to be a prison, to Fisherman's Wharf in San Francisco. No prisoner is believed to have survived the swim, so Mr Le Laune was indeed very fit.

The King of Siam (now Thailand) who came to the throne in 1851 had 82 children by 32 wives.

 Fräulein Brunhilde was the world's tallest pianist: she was said to be 2.10 metres tall. Among the places she performed was the Coliseum Theatre in London.

 Wilt Chamberlain, who was a great basketball star in the USA in the 1970s, was 2.16 metres tall. His parents were only 1.73 metres tall!

 There are up to 8 million hairs on a normal body.

 In Britain in August 1994 twins Spencer and Whitley Horn were born three weeks apart.

A woman's tears are one of the strongest natural antiseptics.

 The bubonic plague is spread by bites from the fleas of black rats. The flea can live without food for 125 days. The bubonic plague has not disappeared. Outbreaks have occurred in America, India, Zimbabwe and South Africa in recent years.

 The tallest woman whose height has been proven was Jane Bunford. She was born in England in 1895. She was 7 foot 7 inches tall. If she did not have a curved spine, she would have been 7 foot 11 inches tall. Her hair also broke records – it was 8 foot long. How often she washed it is not recorded. She died at the age of 27 in 1922.

 A pregnant woman has a one in ninety chance of having twins.

Humans cry from the time they are born until they die. It is a slow tear that cleans the eyeballs and stops them drying out When we blink this water is spread to protect the eyes. On average we blink 25 times a minute.

 Three quarters of human blood is water. We can lose 3 pints of blood without harm. An average adult has between 9 and 12 pints of blood.

 Twins are often ill at the same time, even if they are miles apart. In September 1996 twins Barbara Gamblin and Sue Sycamore, aged 45, were taken to the same hospital at the same time on the same day after separate accidents. Twins' teeth also decay or fall out at much the same time.

Ambulances were first developed by the surgeon to Napoleon during his Italian campaign of 1796–7.

 The tallest people in the world are the men of the Watutsi tribe of central Africa; they grow up to 2.3 metres tall.

 The smallest human being ever known to be born alive was Tyler Davidson, at Nottingham City hospital in 1992. He weighed 11 ounces and was only 15 cm long! He was born two months before he was due and was one of twins; his brother's name was Stephen.

 Over fifty years ago a tribe called the Veddas were found in Sri Lanka. They never laughed.

Burning old shoes was one method of warding off the plague in the 17th century. It did not work.

 A woman who lived in London during the 18th century was so afraid of catching cold she never washed. Instead she smeared her face and hands with lard. She lived to be 116 years old.

 The human stomach can deal with many unusual things being eaten without the person being sick. Some people have set records for eating strange things. The most extreme case is that of Frenchman Michel Lotito. He ate the whole of a Cessna light aircraft, finishing on Boxing Day 1996.

 A giraffe has the same number of bones in its neck as a human does.

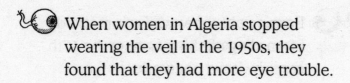 When women in Algeria stopped wearing the veil in the 1950s, they found that they had more eye trouble.

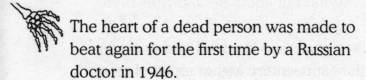 The heart of a dead person was made to beat again for the first time by a Russian doctor in 1946.

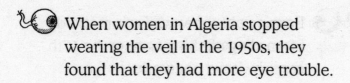 Lady Wergall, the daughter of an English multimillionaire, was frightened of having an anaesthetic for an operation on her knee. In the end she refused to have the operation. As a result she spent 18 years chained to a chair so she would not fall over.

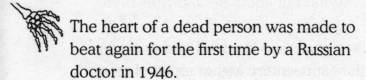 Chinese or Asian people have up to 30,000 more hairs on their heads than white people with red hair. A natural blonde has about 20,000 more hairs on his or her head than an Asian.

People can survive unknown injuries for many years. Joy Connor, an Englishwoman, had a broken neck for 45 years without knowing it. She only found out about her injury in 1996.

 Scotland has the highest proportion of red-headed people in the world. Eleven per cent of the population has red hair.

 Everyone has dandruff. No one yet knows why it happens.

 The famous French scientist Louis Pasteur was not a doctor. He was a chemist and studied germs. He found that germs are carried in the air. His discovery led to the pasteurization of milk, where the harmful germs in milk are killed off. Later he found the vaccines for two diseases, anthrax and rabies.

People have electricity inside them. Some of this can be seen as "static" electricity. In the dark when taking off something synthetic, the blue sparks of this electricity can be seen. Some people have more electricity in their bodies than others. A woman in England had so much she ruined anything electric, including 25 irons, 12 TVs, 3 video recorders and at least 250 lightbulbs.

 In 1988 a man in China was said to have so much electricity in his body he could knock a person down.

 The electricity in an average human body could keep a lightbulb alight for three minutes.

 Sixty per cent of a human body is water – about 10 gallons altogether. The water is about one sixth of a person's weight.

One of the most deadly human diseases is typhoid. One warm day in New York, in 1906, a cook made soup and prepared oysters for guests at a holiday home. The guests seemed to enjoy the meal. But, ten days later, a number of them fell ill and had to go to hospital. A Dr George Soper was called in to investigate. After some time he found that it was the cook, Mary Mallon, who had given the guests the disease. By then Mary had changed jobs several times and wherever she worked someone had caught typhoid. A search for her began. The doctor eventually tracked her down at work. Mary chased him with a rolling pin and then slammed the door in his face. Alarmed, the doctor called in several policemen and they went to Mary's lodgings, where she was taken into custody. She was sent to a hospital for tests. These tests proved that she had given the disease to at least 27 people. In 1910 she was allowed out of hospital, provided she did not work in a kitchen or with food. Yet, five years

35

later "Typhoid Mary" was at it again. Twenty-five nurses and workers at a New York hospital fell ill and again Mary was found, working in the kitchen. She was taken by the police and put into hospital. Mary herself remained unaffected by the disease she carried and died, aged 70, in a New York hospital.

 During the night a human body grows by about a centimetre. It goes back to normal size during the day.

 From the age of 40, people will shrink by about 50 millimetres every 10 years.

In 1890 a Swedish man needed money. He decided to sell his body to the Swedish Institute. He was given the money he wanted. In 1910 he was delighted to find he had been left a large sum of money in a will. Now he wanted to buy his body back. The Swedish Institute said he could not. So the man went to court After hearing him, the court said he could not buy his body back. Not only that, he had to pay money to the Institute. This was because he had had two teeth taken out without letting the Institute know!

 A mother in Sydney, Australia, gave birth to twins 56 days apart and in two different years. The first twin was born on 16 December 1952 and the other on 10 February 1953.

Japanese soldier Nagoaka died aged 75 in 1933. For fifty years he had grown a moustache, which grew and grew. When his body was about to be cremated, his sons snipped off his giant white moustache, which was over 50 centimetres long, folded it in white silk, laid it on satin in a casket and buried it with full honours.

In the Sherlock Holmes stories, Dr Watson, Holmes's assistant, has a bullet wound. Strangely, in one book the wound is in his shoulder, in another in his leg!

Sleeping sickness is a type of swelling of the brain caused by one or more viruses. In 1932 an American woman, Patricia Maguire, was struck by the disease. Her family found it more and more difficult to wake her up in the morning. When she did wake, she went off to work, but when she came home she began to doze off early in the evening. One night she went to sleep on the subway (underground), missed her stop and was woken by the conductor. She just got home, then fell asleep again. For the next ten days she said nothing about what happened, then fell into a deep sleep. She spent 5 years, 7 months and 12 days asleep until, finally, the disease killed her.

 When people close their eyes or stare into the distance, the brain slows down and relaxes the body.

The ancient Egyptians used to put people to sleep before surgery by hitting them on the head! Later, people were made to drink alcohol until they were completely drunk.

 In 1994 a Mr A. Z. Hamock was buried in Kentucky, USA. He had died in 1948. He had been preserved by his family with a home-made embalming fluid, dressed in his evening clothes, and put on a seat in the family home.

 In Perth, Australia, an 18-month-old boy ate a 30 cm venemous snake by accident; his mother arrived in time to pull the tail from his mouth.

40

Harold Blakley was blind for 11 years. When he had his sight restored, the first thing he said was, "Women's hats are ridiculous!"

 The human body loses enough heat in an hour to boil half a gallon of water.

 If skin is transplanted from one person to another it shrinks and dies. The only time this does not happen is if the two people are identical twins.

 One in 15 Americans were found, in a survey in 1978, to bite their toenails as well as their fingernails!

Lynn Ray Collins was unable to speak for 17 years. In 1989 his speech came back after an accident. He somehow hit his head against a glass door which shattered. Blood gushed out of the cut. As soon as the ambulancemen came to help him, he spoke to them!

The amount of iron in a human body is about the same as the iron in a 2.5 cm nail.

Many years ago the Empress of Japan lost her voice. Why she could no longer speak was a mystery. Then one day, on a visit to a village by the sea, she saw a young boy catching a fish on the seashore. She was very impressed and all of a sudden began to speak to him! No one could explain why her voice came back.

It is impossible to sneeze and keep your eyes open at the same time. A 17-year-old girl from Miami, Florida, started to sneeze on 4 January 1966 and continued until 8 June 1966.

 The inventor of the cultured pearl, Mokimoto of Japan, ate two pearls for breakfast each morning.

 The smallest player in major league baseball in the USA was Eddie Gaedel, born in 1925. He appeared as a pitch hitter for the St Louis Browns team against the Detroit Tigers on 19 August 1951. He was only 1.10 metres tall.

Quite often human babies will not grow for up to 63 days and then grow quickly. They then grow up to 1.5 centimetres in a day. Just before babies grow like this they get very hungry and can be very noisy.

An American, Mrs Kemp, had two sets of twins in the same year. Another American had 6 sets of twins over her life!

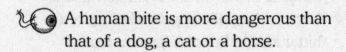 A human bite is more dangerous than that of a dog, a cat or a horse.

The city with the highest number of babies born in taxis is New York, USA.

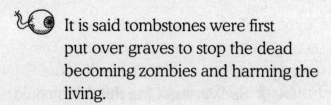 It is said tombstones were first put over graves to stop the dead becoming zombies and harming the living.

 In adults, hair will grow for about three years, then rest for three months. At this time any loose hair falls out.

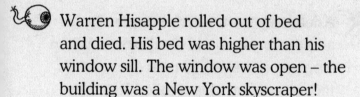 Warren Hisapple rolled out of bed and died. His bed was higher than his window sill. The window was open – the building was a New York skyscraper!

 In 1986 it was found that men and women from Wales have the smallest feet in Britain.

45

Sir Winston Churchill often could not sleep. To help him go to sleep he would have two beds in a room. If he could not sleep on one, he would move to the other. At home, he had one or more pets on his bed, including dogs, cats and a cockatoo.

 Asleep, a person will dream clearly about every one and a half hours. When a person is dreaming, their eyes can move very fast. This is called Rapid Eye Movement, or REM. The American rock band REM is named after this. People take an average of seven minutes to fall asleep.

In an average life a person will eat 50 tonnes of food and drink 50,000 litres of liquid.

Human lungs hold between 3 and 4.5 litres of air.

Tattooing is very ancient. Probably the strangest tattoo ever was found on the arm of a dead man on a streetcar in Cincinatti, USA, in 1946. It read "lykrinxs zerakomp-Baaa-Hobokob-Ahnep-1909"! No one knew what it meant.

The 19th-century violinist Paganini had a hand span (the measure between the tip of the thumb and the tip of the little finger) of 45 centimetres. An average man's hand span is 22.5 centimetres.

 Queen Elizabeth I had a bath once a month. Sometimes she had a bath in wine. The Empress of France in the 19th century had baths in strawberries. Napoleon's first wife, Josephine, had baths in donkey's milk.

 Bodies can be preserved by embalming or by freezing. Freezing the body is called cryogenics. Among famous people whose bodies have been kept are Lenin and the former head of the Philippines, Ferdinand Marcos. Marcos's body is kept in a fridge.

He was put in an airtight glass casket, clutching a rosary and with made-up face and hands. Chemicals will keep his remains fresh for years. When the coffin of King Charles I of England, who had been beheaded, was opened two hundred years after he died, it was found that his hair, beard, face and blue eyes were preserved. One of the people present took a bit of his hair and one of his bones as souvenirs. King Charles I was not very tall: even when he had his head, he was only 1.40 metres.

 The second hand on a watch was invented by a doctor, Sir John Floyer, about 300 years ago, so doctors could check a person's heartbeat.

The great American runner Jesse Owens beat a racehorse over a 100-yard sprint in 1936.

The first American President, George Washington, had three sets of false teeth – one of wood, one of iron and one of ivory. He found the ivory false teeth useless for chewing, but they did taste nice – he kept them in a glass of port every night to improve their flavour.

When a baby is born it has about 305 bones. As it grows some of these bones join together, until there are about 206 left. The main part of the body where joining of bones takes place is the skull.

Shaving can be expensive. When Louis VII of France had his beard and head shaved, his wife thought he looked stupid and left him for a count who was to be Henry II of England. As a result Louis went to war with England. The war lasted almost 300 years and around three million people were killed.

An American man survived and was able to eat six days after being almost cut in half by a circular saw while at work. This was amazing since five important parts of his body had been sliced by the saw in the accident.

51

A very small number of people are born who feel no pain at all. They are very unlucky, and can hurt themselves easily.

 Some people are born with extra toes. The Queen of England has a picture by the famous Dutch painter De Hooch which shows a woman's bare feet. The woman has six toes on one foot. Anne Boleyn, the second wife of Henry VIII, had an extra finger on one of her hands.

Flat feet, where most of the sole touches the ground when standing up, are common. People with flat feet can often walk or stand for longer than those who have normal feet. Oddly, armies have often excused people with flat feet, even though they might be able to stand, march and drill for longer than other soldiers!

 Twins Augusta and Elfried Sejval of Austria had exactly the same fingerprints.

 Like the British writer Charles Dickens, Alexandre Dumas, the French writer of *The Three Musketeers*, found it hard to sleep. He had what is called insomnia. A doctor said he should eat an apple a day at seven o'clock in the morning under the Arc de Triomphe in Paris to be cured. This did not work.

There are over 600 muscles in the body. They are all used for different actions. At least twelve muscles are needed to pick up a pencil, seventeen to smile and 200 pairs to walk.

Mrs Davina Thompson was the first person to have a triple transplant, of her heart, liver and lungs, at Papworth Hospital in Cambridge in 1986.

Englishman John Clogg has an unusual brain. It does not work from one side to the other, which is normal, but each half works on its own. Because of this he can write with both his left and right hands at the same time. He can also speak while writing in this way. He says having such a brain is not really much use. President Garfield of the USA had the same type of brain. He could write Latin with one hand and Greek with the other at the same time.

54

Two men claimed to be the "world's smallest man" at the Kentucky State Fair in America in 1980. Ricki Donovan was 89 centimetres high, but Pete Moore was only 71 centimetres. Ricki refused to change his mind, although it was obvious that Pete was 18 centimetres shorter than he was!

 From the age of 18 to 60 a man who shaves every day will spend a total of 106 days doing so. In bright light if a man has not shaved recently, there is a dark look to the face from the bristles. This is called the "five o'clock shadow". In 1960 Richard Nixon (who later became President of the United States) is said to have lost the election to President Kennedy because, on TV, it looked like he had not shaved.

The great English painter Constable, famous for the Hay Wain, is believed to have had colour blindness. He was, it seems, unable to see red and green clearly. Because of this the greens and reds in his pictures of the countryside are very bright. Colour blindness is passed on to children by their mother.

 Mrs James of New Orleans, USA, sat on a needle when she was a little girl. The needle seemed to disappear inside her. Over twenty years later she felt a pain in her heart. She was rushed to hospital for an emergency operation. The doctor took out a large needle which was close to her heart – it was the one she had sat on years ago.

Teeth are protected by enamel. At the bottom of the teeth there is no enamel, so the gums protect them from decay.

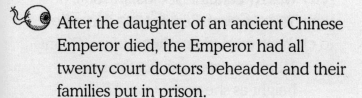 After the daughter of an ancient Chinese Emperor died, the Emperor had all twenty court doctors beheaded and their families put in prison.

 About 2.5 litres of fluid is lost from a person's body each day – over 900 litres a year!

General Tom Thumb, whose real name was Charles Stratton, was the most famous American midget. He was born in 1838. At the age of 12 he was only 77 centimetres tall.

57

He joined P. T. Barnum's Museum in America in 1842 and went on show. He travelled in America, Britain and Europe for three years. He married Lavinia Warren, who was 81 centimetres tall, in 1863. The General died in 1883. His wife then married another midget, Count Magi, who was exactly the same height as she was.

 Richard III of England, Louis XIV of France and the Emperor Napoleon of France were all born with teeth.

 The Danish astronomer Tycho Brahe, who died in 1601, had a gold false nose. He lost his real nose in a sword fight.

Eyelashes do not turn white as we get older. Each eyelash lasts about 5 months. It is thought, though not proven, that some people's hair, including their eyebrows, turns white very quickly after a big shock. A British soldier who went to the front line in the First World War in 1914 had such a fright. One day, he was throwing a grenade, when it went off early. It blew off two of his own fingers and killed a man near him. The shock seemed to make his hair turn white in days.

One in ten people is left-handed. Prince William is left-handed. His great-grandfather, King George VI, was born left-handed but was taught to write with his right hand. No one knows why, but left-handed people die younger than right-handed people. Other famous left-handed people include the artists Picasso and Michelangelo and the early film star

Charles Chaplin. When typing, the left hand does fifty-six per cent of the work. Oddly, the number of left-handed men is double the number of left-handed women.

The man who first studied the human body in the West, Vesalius, had to study dead bodies at night. Mostly they were the bodies of people who had been executed. He was once accused of cutting up a Spaniard while he was still alive. Although he was able to show this was untrue, the court of the Inquisition said he had to make a pilgrimage to Jerusalem. During the journey his ship was wrecked. Vesalius made it to a desert island, but he died there of starvation.